Wedding

PLANNING GUIDE

A BRIDES WORKBOOK

Wedding
PLANNING GUIDE
A BRIDES WORKBOOK

TANYA PORTER

ARPress
ILLUMINATING IDEAS
EMPOWERING VOICES

ARPress
45 Dan Road Suite 5
Canton MA 02021
Hotline: 1(888) 821-0229
Fax: 1(508) 545-7580

Ordering Information:

Quantity sales. Special discounts are available on quantity purchases by corporations, associations, and others. For details, contact the publisher at the address above.

Printed in the United States of America.

ISBN-13:   Softcover   979-8-89356-613-0

              eBook   979-8-89356-614-7

Library of Congress Control Number: 2024903639

Table Of Contents

CONGRATULATIONS on your upcoming wedding! You have many happy hours and days ahead of you as you plan this most important day.

Whether you are inviting 50 or 500 guests to your wedding, it takes a lot or organization to have a smooth flowing event. You will have many decisions to make. **The WEDDING PLANNING GUIDE** will make that job a lot easier as it is designed to keep you organized. The hardest part of getting started in your planning process is knowing where to start. This guide will take you from setting up your budget to planning the transportation of your out of town guests. The format, that of a working notebook, makes it easy to take with you to appointments and keep all your clippings for ideas and information together.

Don't let yourself get overwhelmed. Start by asking friends, family or your wedding coordinator for referrals of vendors. Limit yourself to three in each category. If after interviewing these three you don't find one that suits your needs, go on to the next three. This will keep each category manageable and less stressful for you.

Interviewing vendors is very important. This gives you the opportunity to meet face to face and to see their work and ask questions. Do they listen to what you want? Are they within your budget? Do you feel comfortable with them? After all, this is one of the most important events in your life and you want everything as close to perfect as possible.

Look in books and magazines for ideas for cakes, flowers, decorating ideas. Don't limit yourself to just typical wedding ideas, develop your own. A coordinator can help you do this as can a good caterer and florist. Dare to dream! This is your day, the day when all your dreams and fantasies are fulfilled.

FORWARD
A WORD ABOUT WEDDING COORDINATORS

You just got engaged! You are excited with anticipation of a wedding that you've dreamed about since you were a little girl. Then you discover, during the planning process, there are as many frustrating moments ahead.

An early question usually is, do I need a coordinator or should I pursue the route of a consultant and/or the usual barrage of advice? A consultant is an experienced person who answers questions and gives you guidance. A coordinator not only answers questions, gives guidance, but follows through with implementation.

If you answer yes to any of the following questions, you probably need a coordinator.

1) Do I need help establishing a budget?
2) Do I need assistance in planning my wedding to stay within the budget?
3) Do I need assistance in finding quality/proven vendors?
4) Do I need someone to help me save precious time?
5) Do I need help in negotiations with family and/or vendors?
6) Do I want to be stress free on my wedding day?
7) Do I live away from the area where we want to get married?
8) Do we want our family and friends to enjoy our wedding day without the hassle of solving potential problems?

If I hire a coordinator will he/she take over? NO! This is **YOUR** wedding. A coordinator offers experienced based advice but is guided by you through each step, listening to what you and your family want. The coordinator helps you get started, is a# confidant and a mediator, but most of all a friend. A coordinator will save you time, money and most of all needless stress.

The best reason for using a coordinator, is to allow you and your family the enjoyment of the planning process as well as your wedding day. You and your family will arrive at the wedding with little to do but enjoy **YOUR** day to the fullest.

Your coordinator, will work closely with you. They will be as involved in the entire process as you wish them to be, answering questions, helping with decisions, contracts, and offering suggestions to make your day as perfect as it can be.

Your coordinator will be there to choreograph the rehearsal, be a background attendant, executing your plans at the wedding and your reception if you choose, minimizing disappointments and disruptions for a smooth, flowing event.

WHO IS WEDDINGS ETC. LLC And WHY DID THIS BOOK COME ABOUT?

In 1991, Tanya Porter started as a wedding coordinator for Hope United Methodist Church, in Englewood, Colorado.

This naturally evolved into WEDDINGS, ETC. LLC!

Tanya has helped numerous brides realize their wedding day dreams by relieving them and their mothers, of the stress of coordinating the rehearsal, wedding and reception.

As a coordinator, her job has been that of counselor, confidant and jack of all trades. By taking over the coordination of your special day, it allows you and your family some very special memories. Being there to pin on corsages, boutonnieres, making sure the church is decorated and everyone is dressed properly and ready to go is just part of the job description of a coordinator. A coordinator will make sure the ushers know what to do and that everyone is aware of protocol and what's expected of them. If the ring bearer decides not to go down the aisle, she/he makes sure the rings do!

While doing research for brides, it came to Tanya's attention that there are volumes of information in the market, but what a bride (or her mother) needs is a way to categorize and keep the information together and close at hand. Out of these findings was born the **WEDDING PLANNING GUIDE**. Keep it close at hand for those magazine pictures you find of flowers, cakes, favors, and ideas you discover. Use it as the workbook you need to keep you organized and on track. Utilize it in conjunction with your coordinator.

Best wishes and GOOD LUCK in your planning process!

Sincerely,

Tanya W. Porter
Managing Member
WEDDINGS,ETC.LLC

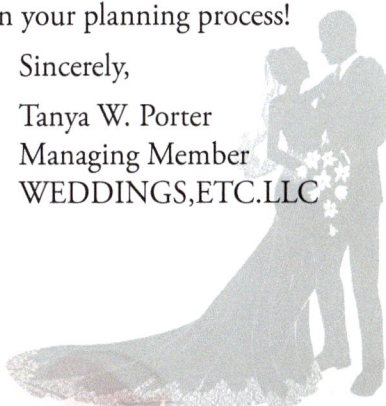

Location of Wedding_____

Wedding Date_____Rehearsal Date_____

Wedding Time_____Rehearsal Time _____

Reception Location_____

WHO PAYS FOR WHAT?

Bride/family:

Traditionally pays for wedding ceremony and reception.
Contemporary: everyone contributes.

Wedding Consultant/coordinator
Wedding dress, veil, accessories
Invitation, announcements, enclosures, personal stationery, stamps.
Trousseau and lingerie
Bouquets/corsages for attendants
Flowers for ceremony and reception site
Rental fee for church or chapel.
Engagement and wedding photographs.
Fees for sexton, organist or soloists.
Rental fees for aisle carpet and other equipment.
Transportation of bridal party to the ceremony and reception sites.
Complete receptions. All food, beverages, music, decorations, gratuities, and other services.
Grooms ring.
Wedding gift for groom
Gifts for the bride's attendants.
Hotel lodging for any attendants and friends from out-of-town.
Gratuities to parking attendants.
Bridesmaid's luncheon.
Corsages for mothers, grandparents, special guests.

Groom/family pays for:
Brides engagement/wedding rings.
Marriage License.
Ceremony official's fee
Bride's flowers (bouquet and going-away corsage.)
Wedding gift for bride.
Gifts for best man and ushers
Hotel lodging for out-of-town ushers.
Wedding night suite
Rehearsal dinner
Honeymoon
Blood tests

Gloves, ties, and ascots for men in wedding party.

Attendants pay for:

Personal wedding attire.
Personal traveling expenses.

Bachelorette Party

SETTING UP A BUDGET

Description	Est. Cost	Actual Cost	Bride's Family Exp.	Groom's Family Exp.	Bride/Groom Expenses	Other's Expenses
Wedding Coordinator						
Ceremony Site						
Officiant						
Marriage License						
Bride's Attire						
Attendant's Attire						
Groom's Attire						
Groomsmen's Attire						
Flower-girl(s) Attire						
Ring-Bearer(s) Attire						
Mother's Attire						
Father's Attire						
Bride's Ring						
Groom's Ring						
Wedding Stationary including: Save the Date Cards, Invitations, Maps Response Cards, Wedding Programs, Stamps, Thank You's, Brunch Invitations, Announcements, Calligraphy						
Rehearsal Dinner						
Reception Site						
Caterer						
Liquor (Bar)						
Dinner Wine						
Ice Sculpture						
Wedding Cake						
Special Linens						
Wedding Flowers Bouquets, Corsages, Boutonnieres, Altar Flowers, Pew Candle Décor, Pew Décor, Candelabra Flowers, Guest Book Flowers, Flower-girl Baskets, Aisle Runner						
Reception Flowers Table Décor, Cake Table, Buffet Arrangements, Throw-a-way bouquet, etc.						
Rehearsal Dinner Flowers						
Bridesmaid's Luncheon/Brunch						
Gifts for Attendants/Groomsmen/ Parents						
Organist						
Soloist(s)						
DJ						

Band						
Photographer						
Videographer						
Wedding Night Suite						
Honeymoon						
Physical for Bride/Groom						
Blood Tests (HIV/Measles)						
Housing for Special Out of Town Guests						
Gift Baskets for Special Out of Town Guests						
Limo/Carriage						
Make Up/Hair Styling for Bridal Party						
MISCELLANEOUS						
Garter						
Cake Knife and Server						
Guest Book and Pen						
Signature Picture						
Ring Pillow/Chest						
Toasting Glasses						
Bubbles/Birdseed						
Unity Candle and Tapers – Candle Holders						
Doves						
Favors						
Extra Stating (Creates a special look)						
Special Lighting						
Huppah						
Ketubbah						
Broom (For "Jumping the Broom)						
Bouquet Preservation						
Wedding Dress Preservations						
RENTALS						
Tent						
Dance Floor						
Candelabra						

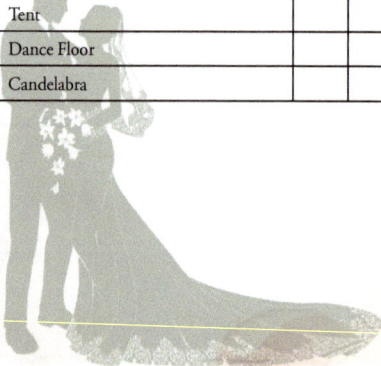

SAMPLE BUDGET BASED ON $20,000 FOR 150 GUESTS

Band COORDINATOR (10-20% of budget)	11%		
WEDDING SITE	3%		
BRIDAL ATTIRE	6%		
GROOM'S ATTIRE	1%		
PHOTOGRAPHY	8%		
VIDOEGRAPHY	7%		
OFFICIATE	1%		
MUSIC	2%		
INVITATIONS/STATIONARY	2%		
FLORIST	7%		
RECEPTION SITE	10%		
CATERING	28%		(DON'T FORGET TO INCLUDE SERVICE CHARGE & TAX
CAKE	2%		
FULL BAR	10%		
BEER/WINE SERVICE	6%		
TRANSPORTATION	3%		
DJ	3%		
BAND	18%		

There will be variables in this budget depending on what's most important to you. Remember this is a guideline to help establish your own working budget.

After you've established the budget, it's a good idea to add another 10% for miscellaneous items you may want to add.

MARRIAGE LICENSE	
GARTER	
GUEST BOOK/PEN	
CAKE KNIFE/SERVER	
FAVORS	
UNITY CANDLE/HOLDERS/TAPERS	
BUBBLES/BIRD-SEED	
RELEASE DOVES	
RING PILLOW/BOX	
TOASTING GLASSES	
ATTENDANTS GIFTS	
SPECIAL GUEST BASKETS	

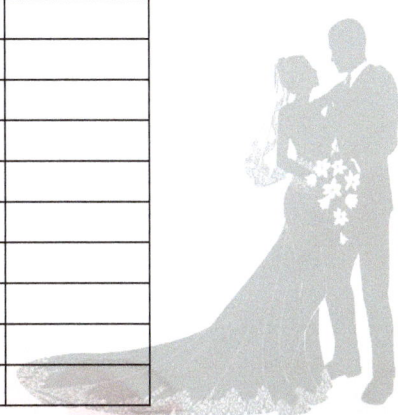

TYPES OF WEDDINGS

Ultraformal (6-12 attendants) 350 plus guests
Always conducted after 6:00 pm

Formal (3-8 attendants) 150 - 350 guests
Late afternoon or early evening.

Semi-formal (1-4 attendants) 100 -150 guests
Late morning or early afternoon wedding.

Informal (1 attendant each) fewer than 50 guests

     One usher for every 50 guests.

     Garden

     Theme

     Morning

     Noon

     Afternoon

     Evening

Who will give bride away?_____

_____   _____

_____   _____

_____   _____

_____   _____

Pages:_____   _____

Flower Girls:_____Ushers:_____

_____   _____

_____   _____

Ring Bearer:_____

Clergy/judge:_____

Photographer: _____

Videographer:_____

Organist/music:_____

_____

Soloist(s):_____

Readers:_____

StringTrio/Quarter:_____

Florist:_____

Candle-lighters:_____

Determine guest list:
1/3 brides parents
1/3 grooms parents
1/3 bride and groom.)

NOTES:

TIME LINE:

Six to Twelve Months:

[ ] Decide budget
[ ] Wedding Coordinator
[ ] Decide type of wedding
[ ] Choose location for ceremony
[ ] Choose attendants (alternate attendants)
[ ] Select gown, veil and accessories
[ ] Purchase undergarments to be worn with wedding gown. (You'll want to wear these at each fitting.)
[ ] Purchase undergarments - Consider having bra cups sewn into the gown
[ ] Select attendants; gowns
[ ] Start to work on your guest list (divide 3 ways between bride/groom/parents) 1/3 Bride and Groom 1/3 to Brides Parents 1/3 Grooms Parents
[ ] Select reception site
[ ] Start to plan reception
[ ] Select men's formalwear
[ ] Select photographer
[ ] Select videographer
[ ] Select and reserve florist
[ ] Select places for bridal registry
[ ] Select music for wedding ceremony (soloists and special musicians)
[ ] Select music for reception
[ ] Start developing your honeymoon plans
[ ] Arrange lodging for out of town guests
[ ] If you need passports for honeymoon, order now
[ ] Reserve Makeup artist
[ ] Reserve Hair Stylist

FOUR MONTHS

[ ] Order invitations, personal stationary and wedding programs
[ ] Mail Save the Date cards
[ ] Finalize honeymoon reservations/plans
[ ] Design maps to be inserted in invitations (wedding/reception)
[ ] Select/make ring cushion

[ ] Reserve Limo/transportation for Bridal Party
[ ] Reserve make-up artist and hair stylist

THREE MONTHS

[ ] Mothers select dresses/gowns.
[ ] Schedule attendant's fittings.
[ ] Bride/Groom get physical check ups/any blood tests.
[ ] Order wedding cake, accessories, and favors(top for cake, knife
    and server. Have engraved.) Order groom's cake.
[ ] Address wedding invitations.
[ ] Reserve Limo/transportation for Bridal Party.

TWO MONTHS

[ ] Mail wedding invitations
[ ] If placing announcements with newspapers, check deadlines
[ ] Select attendants gifts.
[ ] Purchase wedding rings, have sized. Order engraving.
[ ] Reserve rental items necessary

        Rental shop_____

        Phone_____
[ ] Arrange parking attendants if necessary.
[ ] Purchase Bride and Groom's gifts to each other.

ONE MONTH

[ ] Plan a special day with your fiancé to get marriage license. (In
    Colorado license is good for 30 days.) Then go have lunch!
[ ] Have formal wedding portrait taken. (A lot of brides do this at the
    church prior to the ceremony. It's also a good dress rehearsal to try
    out your hair style, makeup and practice walking in your dress.)
[ ] Arrange for ice sculptures (if caterer/hotel isn't handling.)

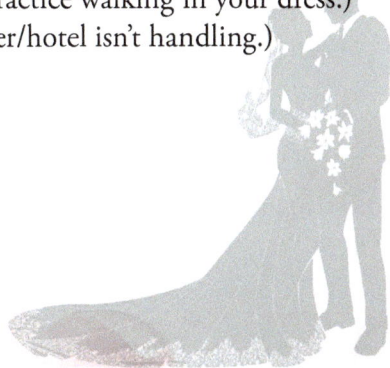

ITEM_____

[ ] Confirm honeymoon reservations. Check luggage. (Do you need any new pieces?)

[ ] Arrange for final fitting of your gown. (Be sure to take undergarmentsfor this fitting.)

[ ] Remind bridesmaids of final gown fittings. (Attendants should have their shoes and any special undergarments necessary with them for this fitting.)

[ ] Double check attire and accessories for all members of the wedding party. (Be sure that any shoes or special accessories that may have been ordered are in. If shoes are being dyed, be sure attendants order them in advance so correct color is sent. Have all attendants wear shoes to break them in and scuff up bottoms so they won't slip on carpet when walking down the aisle. Bride should also break in shoes.)

[ ] Check to be sure that all the men's shirt studs are the same.

[ ] If having your hair done for the wedding, try out any new styles now. Take your veil/hair piece with you.

TWO WEEKS

[ ] Record wedding gifts as you receive them and keep up with your thank you notes.

[ ] Confirm time & date of rehearsal with all members of your wedding party.

[ ] Groom/parents confirm reservations for rehearsal dinner.

[ ] Review receptions eating plans and prepare place cards is desired.

[ ] Complete trousseau shopping.

[ ] Schedule hair/nail appointments.

[ ] Arrange for changing your name and address on bank account, credit cards, driver's license, social security.

ONE WEEK

[ ] Final consultations with coordinator, caterer, florist, musicians and photographers.

[ ] Give final guest count to reception facility or caterer [ ] Make final payments.

[ ] Host bridesmaid's brunch/luncheon:

Restaurant:_____

Time:_____

[ ] Begin packing for honeymoon.

RELAX AND GET PLENTY OF REST IT'S TIME TO ENJOY!

The day of the Wedding.

>Arrange with caterer or someone to have something to drink and eat for the couple in their private room.
>Eat something at the reception.
>Have finger food and beverages available in both Bride's and Groom's dressing rooms for wedding party. It's a good idea to have also have hard candy available.
>Eat something at the reception.

>Have the attendants put makeup on before they arrive at the church/wedding site to dress.

>Bride..make up at home or arrange to have make up artist at wedding site. If having hair done prior to arriving at wedding site, wear a button shirt so you won't have to put it over your head.

NOTES:

WEDDING APPOINTMENTS

Appointment with **PASTOR/PRIEST/RABBI/OFFICIANT**

Date_____Time_____

Place_____

Appointment with **WEDDING CONSULTANT**

Date_____Time_____

Place_____

Appointment with **CATERER/RECEPTION SITE**

Date_____Time_____

Place_____

Appointment with **ORGANIST/MUSCIANS**

Date_____Time_____

Place_____

Date_____Time_____

Place_____

Date_____Time_____

Place_____

Music_____

Appointment with **SOLOIST**

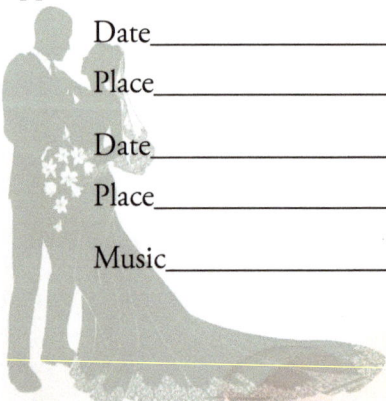

Date_____Time_____

Place_____

Date_____Time_____

Place_____

Music_____

Appointment with **BAKERY** for Wedding Cake and Groom's Cake

Date_____Time_____

Place_____

Date_____Time_____

Place_____

Date_____Time_____

Place_____

Appointment with **BRIDAL SHOP**

Date_____Time_____

Place_____

Date_____Time_____

Place_____

Date_____Time_____

Place_____

FITTING

Date_____Time_____

Place_____

Date_____Time_____

Place_____

FINAL FITTING

Date_____Time_____

Place_____

PICK UP DRESS

Date_____Time_____

Place_____

Appointment with **ENTERTAINMENT**

Date_____Time_____

Place_____

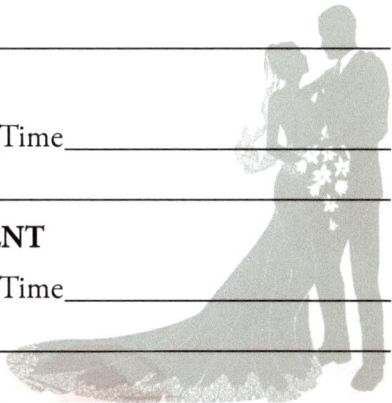

Date_____Time_____

Place_____

Appointment with **FLORIST**

Date_____Time_____

Place_____

Date_____Time_____

Place_____

Appointment with **INVITATIONS/CALLIGRAPHER**

Date_____Time_____

Place_____

Date_____Time_____

Place_____

Appointment with **LIMOUSINE/CARRIAGE SERVICE**

Date_____Time_____

Place_____

Appointment with **HAIR SALON**

Date_____Time_____

Place_____

Hair Designer_____

Appointment with **NAILS**

Date_____Time_____

Place_____

Appointment with **PHOTOGRAPHER**

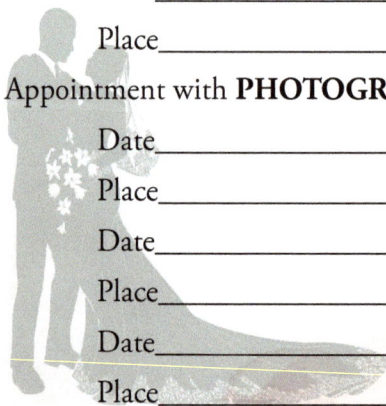

Date_____Time_____

Place_____

Date_____Time_____

Place_____

Date_____Time_____

Place_____

Appointment with **VIDEOGRAPHER**

    Date_____Time_____

    Place_____

    Date_____Time_____

    Place_____

    Date_____Time_____

    Place_____

Appointment with **TUXEDO SHOP**

    Date_____Time_____

    Place_____

    Date_____Time_____

    Place_____

Appointment for **MARRIAGE LICENSE**

    Date_____Time_____

    Place_____

Appointment with your fiancé to set up your gift register

    Date_____Time_____

    Place_____

    Place_____

    Place_____

    Place_____

NOTES:

FLOWERS

Bride's bouquet_____(Will florist comp throw-a-way bouquet? Will florist dry flowers and make into an arrangement?)

Preservation of bouquet_____

Who is responsible for delivery_____

Take a swatch of fabric from attendants dresses to match to flowers. Also a picture of the wedding dress and attendants dress will help in selecting style of bouquets to order. Take a swatch of fabric from attendants dresses to match to flowers. Also a picture of the wedding dress and attendants dress will help in selecting style of bouquets to order.

Maid/Matron of Honor's bouquet:_____

Attendants' flowers:_____

Hairpieces:_____

Pew floral arrangements/bows/candles_____

Alter/other arrangements:_____

Beauty baskets:_____

Candelabra arrangements (bows/flowers)_____

Flower-girl(s) basket(s)_____

Flower-girl(s) hairpiece(s):_____

Aisle carpet:_____

Who will attach?_____

Who will roll out?_____

(Usually it's a good idea to fasten it down ahead of time and usher guests down outside aisles. This way it will be secure.

CORSAGES:

Mother of Bride_____

Mother of Groom_____

Step-mother of Bride_____

Step-mother of Groom_____

Grandmother(s) of Bride_____

Grandmother(s) of Groom_____
(Any other special friends/relatives.)
Godmother:_____

Guest Book Attendant:_____

Gifts for Attendants:_____

(Single roses to present mothers.)_____
(Single roses to present as first gifts as husband and wife)_____
Boutonnieres

Groom:_____
Best Man:_____
Groomsmen: _____
Ushers:_____
RingBearer:_____

Father of Bride:_____
Father of Groom:_____
Stepfather of Bride:_____
Stepfather of Groom:_____
Grandfather(s) of Bride:_____
Grandfather(s) of Groom:_____
Godfather:_____

Any special people:(ex. clergy if friend or relative):_____

Cake Table_____
Cakeknife_____
Gift Table/guest book table:(Can use throw-a-way bouquet for guest
book table_____
Center Pieces:_____
Buffet tables:_____

NOTES:_____
_____
_____
_____
_____

Stationary Items:

Save the Date Cards:

Invitations:

Stamps: (You need stamps for Save the Date cards, Invitations, Response Cards, and Thank You Notes)_____

_____

Maps:_____

Calligraphy:_____

Response Cards:_____

Thank you notes:_____

Announcements:_____

Programs for Wedding:_____

PlaceCards:_____

Cake Napkins with name and date engraved on them:_____

_____

Match covers engraved with name:_____

Favors:_____

Toasting goblets:_____

Cake knife/server: Bride's Book:_____

Guest book/pen:_____

Unity Candle/tapers: (With or without candle holders.)

Miscellaneous:
Bubbles/confetti/birdseed/balloons etc to be thrown at reception:
Card Box:_____

Assign someone to take care of the card box until it can be given to a designated person after the reception..

Items to be rented for Wedding ceremony: Chairs, Kneeling bench, Arch, Canopy, Aisle Runner, Candelabra and lighters, Special Linens, China, Crystal, etc.

Items to be rented for reception:

Rental store:_____
_____
_____

BRIDE AND ATTENDANTS ATTIRE:

Chosen colors:_____

Bride's Wedding gown:_____
_____

(When measuring for gown, be sure to use a good, vinyl tape measure. Be sure the dress is ordered in your size to avoid costly alterations.)

Shop:_____
Date ordered:_____
Fitting:_____
Alterations if necessary:_____
Pressing:_____
Date to be picked up:_____

Slip:_____
Special underwear:_____
Shoes:_____
Garter:_____
Nylons:_____
Coin for shoe:_____

Veil:_____

Date ordered if necessary:_____

Deposit:_____

Balance Due:_____

Trousseau:_____
_____
_____
_____

Attendants attire:
(When picking out attendants dresses, try to get something they can possibly wear again and that is well made. If short on time, you may want to consider looking at local department stores as well as bridal shops. They may be able to order what you want or find them at other stores. These dresses are more apt to be worn again and money better spent.) If attendants are from out of town, have them visit a local bridal

shop to be measured. They then need to send the measurements to you for ordering the dresses. This is done to assure all the dresses are cut from the same dye lot.

Dress:_____

_____

Shoes:_____

_____

Accessories:_____

_____

Hair ornaments/flowers:_____

_____

Additional Jewelry:_____

Gloves: Long_____Short_____Color_____

Flowergirl(s)dress:_____

Bride's Mother's dress:_____

Bride's Step-mother's dress: _____

Groom's Mother's dress: _____

Groom's Step-mother's dress: _____

NOTES:

GROOM and GROOMSMEN'S ATTIRE

Tux Shop:_____

Groom:_____

_____

Shirt:_____

Tie:_____

Vest or cummerbund:_____

Shoes:_____

Accessories:_____

If the groomsmen are from out of town, have them measured at a local tux shop and mail the measurements to you. You then need to take them to your local tux shop to reserve the attire.

Best Man:_____

_____

Groomsmen:_____

_____

_____

Ushers:_____

_____

_____

RingBearer:_____

_____

Fathers:_____

_____

_____

Grandfathers:_____

NOTES:

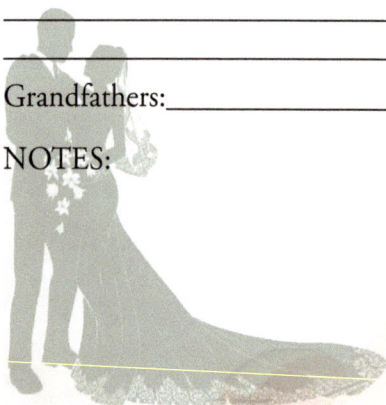

PHOTOGRAPHER

COMPANY:_____

ADDRESS:_____

PHONE:_____

DEPOSIT:_____

BALANCE DUE:_____

Does the photographer use one or two people for coverage?_____
Ask to be shown an album of one complete wedding to get an overall feeling for their work.

**Suggested Photographer's check list of wedding candid shots.
(Each photographer will also have a list of suggestions.)**
Before the Ceremony:

Bride in dress	Bride at gift table
Bride with mother	Bride leaving house
Bride with father	Bride and father in car
Bride with both parents	Groom alone
Bride with step parents	Groom with best man
Bride with honor attendant	Ushers getting boutonnieres
Bride with grandparents	Bride touching up make-up
Everyone getting flowers	Parent's signing guestbook
Groom with parents	Bride with parents

Father putting coin in bride's shoe; For goodluck

At the Ceremony:

Guests outside church	Maid/matron of honor
Bride and father getting out of car	Flower girl/ring bearer
Bride and father going into church	Bride and father/mother
Ushers escorting guests	Groom meeting bride
Groom's parents being seated	The Kiss
Soloist and organist	Bride and groom in recess.
Groom and ushers at alter	Bride and groom and guests
Giving-away ceremony (if allowed)	Bride and groom in car

Bride/groom exchanging vows (if allowed) Bride and groom & families
Ring ceremony (if allowed)
Bridesmaids coming down aisle

The reception room   Bride/Groom saying good-bye
Parent's table   Guests throwing birdseed/blowing bubbles
Bride/Groom dancing   Limo speeding off
Bride/father dancing   Cake table
Groom/mother dancing   Other reception fun
The musicians   Bride/Groom cutting cake
Bride/Groom talking with guests   Bride/Groom with Coordinator

NOTES:

VIDEOGRAPHER

COMPANY:_____

ADDRESS:_____

PHONE:_____

DEPOSIT:_____

BALANCE DUE:_____

Does Videographer use one, two or more cameras or a drone?

Have them show you the difference in quality utilizing more than one camera.

When choosing your photographer and videographer, remember that when the reception is over, what you have left besides your memories will be your pictures. Choose someone you feel totally comfortable with.

NOTES:

CUSTOMARY RESPONSIBILITIES

Maid/Matron/Man of Honor

Helps address envelopes if not using calligrapher.
Makes sure all attendants are dressed perfectly, including all accessories.
Witness and signs the marriage certificate.
Precedes the bride and her father down aisle.
Arranges the veil and train at the alter.
Passes grooms ring.
Sits to the left of the groom at the bride's table.
Helps bride change into going away clothes.
If there are both a maid of honor and matron of honor:
> * They share the responsibilities listed above.
> * Best man escorts Matron of honor.
> * Head usher escorts maid of honor.

Helps record gifts.

BEST MAN or BEST WOMAN

Signs and produces the marriage certificate at appropriate time.
Carries bride's wedding ring.
Makes sure ushers are properly dressed and briefed about ceremony procedures and their responsibilities.
Pays clergyman.
Toastmaster at the reception:
Sits to the right of the bride at the bride's table.
Proposes first toast to the couple.
Reads telegrams/letters aloud if bride and groom wish.
Makes sure the reception goes as planned with no practical jokes. Helps groom get going-away clothes together.
Makes sure clothes are locked in truck of car or checked in ahead of time. Makes sure all men's rental clothes are returned to the formal-wear store.
Deposits any money gifts received at the wedding in appropriate accounts.

USHERS

Seat guests at the ceremony.

Rule of thumb: One usher for every 50 guests.

Before wedding:

Offer female guests right arm.

Except for elder men, men follow escort down aisle.

Bride's guests are seated on left side.

Groom's guests are seated on right side.

When bride or groom has more guests than the other, seat all guests together.

Eldest woman should be escorted first should a party arrive in a group.

Mother of groom is seated about five minutes before mother of the bride.

After the mother of the bride is seated, processional begins and no guests should be seated.

May unfold the aisle carpet.

After the wedding:
Take care of aisle carpet.
Escort first the mother of the bride out.
Escort the mother of the groom out.
Face the pew and signal guests to file out row by row.

At the reception:

Encourage single men and to participate in garter ceremony.

Bride's Mother

Guest list for bride's side
Can help with planning.
Helps select wedding dress.
Helps keep track of gifts.
Displays gifts in an attractive and safe spot.

Informs groom's mother of her wedding attire choice so dresses will be same length and accessorized the same way. Official hostess for wedding.
Last person seated at wedding ceremony. Seated on left hand side of aisle. (Seated on right side if Jewish ceremony.)
First person escorted out after recessional
Greets guests at the head of the receiving line.
Sits in a place of honor at the parent's table.
Encourages single women and men to participate in bouquet and garter ceremonies.
May escort bride down aisle.

Bride's Father

Guest list (if divorced)
Rides to ceremony with bride.
Escorts bride down aisle.
Attire should blend with groom's and usher's attire.

Groom's Parents

Guest list for groom's side
Mother should select attire that compliments bride's mother's attire.

Discuss with future daughter-in-law what she will call you.
Make accommodations for out of town guests (grooms).
Give rehearsal dinner.
Head usher escorts parents down the aisle and seats them on the right front pew. (Left for Jewish weddings)

In the receiving line:

Stand between bride and bride's mother
Groom's mother stands next to the bride's mother
Groom's father stand next to bride.
Act as host/hostess at reception.
Encourage guests to dance, single men and women to participate in bouquet and garter ceremonies.

If divorced, groom's mother sits in first pew at ceremony, and groom's father sits in second or third pew.

NOTES:

ADDITIONAL RESPONSIBILITIES:

[ ] Person to bustle the bride's train.

If this person is someone besides your coordinator, take them with you for your Final fitting. Have them draw a map to show where the hooks are for your bustle. This will save you a lot of time when bustling your dress.

[ ] Person responsible for all tips, etc. (This can be handled by wedding coordinator if desired.)

[ ] Person responsible for checks to pay last minute bills. (Put into envelopes and give to your coordinator to distribute.)

[ ] Person responsible to taking flowers to reception site:

[ ] Person responsible for having Bride's bouquet preserved:

[ ] Person responsible for giving flowers to bridal party and guests and for pinning on corsages and boutonnieres: (Usually this is done by your coordinator or florist)

[ ] Person responsible for taking guest book to reception:

[ ] Person responsible for taking gifts to reception:

[ ] Person(s) responsible for taking gifts home after reception:

[ ] Person(s) responsible for flowers after reception:

[ ] Person responsible for retrieving wedding cake and top:

[ ] Person responsible for getting newly weds to airport:

[ ] Person responsible for house sitting during festivities:

[ ] Person(s)responsible for gift table/card box:

[ ] Person responsible for gift checks:

[ ] Person responsible for getting bride's/groom's luggage to honeymoon suite.

NOTES:

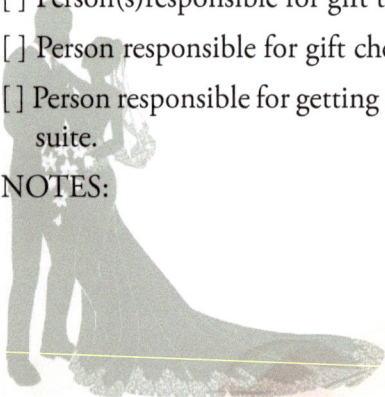

SPECIAL BRUNCHES/LUNCHEONS/DINNERS

Rehearsal Dinner

Given by Groom's family (or may be sponsored by bride's family).

Guests include:
Members of wedding party
Bride's parents Groom's parents
Clergyman and spouse
Musicians (if they attend rehearsal)
Out of town guests (optional)
Spouses of bridal party (optional)

Usually takes place after rehearsal. This can be any type of get together from an informal coffee and cake to a bar-b- que to a more formal dinner. The object of the rehearsal dinner is for the families to become better acquainted.

Wedding Day Breakfast or Lunch

Hosted by friend, relative, or neighbor.

Out-of-town guests are invited. Purpose is to entertain guests on wedding day while bride and groom and immediate family take care of last-minute details.

Bride and groom are not expected to attend.

(It's best to have parties several days before the wedding. This eliminates hangovers or upset stomachs for the wedding.)

Bachelor Party:_____

_____

Rehearsal Dinner: (Who do you wish to include?)

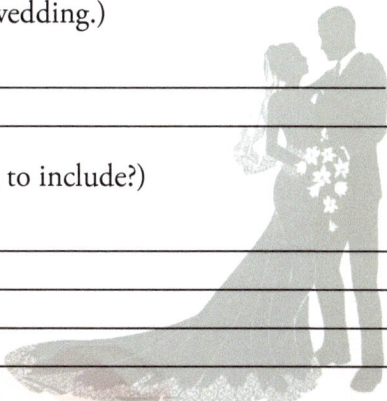

_____

_____

_____

Bridesmaids Brunch/Luncheon:
Where to have it? Do you need to make reservations?

Special plans for out of town guests for AFTER the wedding...
Morning after brunch:

Transportation from Wedding site to Reception site.

Who will be riding with Bride and Groom? Will you need more than one conveyance? Who will drive?

Own Car:_____

Who will drive?_____

Limo- Company_____

Time to arrive?_____

Horse/Carriage-Company:_____

Time to arrive?_____

Antique Car-Company:_____

Time to arrive?_____

Who will drive?_____

TRANSPORTATION FROM RECEPTION TO START OF HONEYMOON

How to get from reception to airport/railroad etc. Time you need to leave

_____

Parking:_____

Valet:_____

NOTES

THE CEREMONY

When selecting a venue for your ceremony, decide if you want a house of worship, to do it outdoors, or at the same venue as the reception. For budgetary reasons, many brides prefer to get married at the same place as the reception. Many venues are set up for both and usually can offer another area, away from where the actual reception will be held for the ceremony. Always have a back up if having your ceremony/reception outdoors.

WHAT TYPE OF CEREMONY?

Do you want to invite all the guests to your ceremony and to the reception?_____

_____

Is the ceremony going to be more intimate with only family and close friends attending? _____

_____

WHERE TYPE OF CEREMONY?

Venue: _____

_____

If outside, back up site in case of bad weather?_____

_____

_____

Is venue air conditioned? [ ] Yes [ ] No
Some of the older churches, generally 100 years or older, may not have air conditioning. Take this into consideration when selecting the time of year you want to get married if you are looking at one of these churches.

Adequate heating? [ ] Yes [ ] No

Sound system? [ ] Yes [ ] No Who will operate it? _____

_____

How many guests will the venue hold? _____

_____

Is there adequate parking?_____

If not, is there a commercial parking lot you might be able to rent?
_____

Center or side aisle?_____

Number of pews: _____

If using an aisle runner, length of aisle: _____

If you are not getting married in a house of worship, do you need to rent chairs? [ ] Yes [ ] No

Number of chairs needed?_____ Type of chair?_____
décor?_____

Who will you rent from if this is necessary?_____

Day and time to be delivered?_____

Who is responsible for setting up and taking down the chairs? ___
_____

> If you are having your ceremony and reception at the same site, the caterers will usually take care of setting up and taking down the chairs for you. Be sure to ask them if they will.

Officiant _____
_____

If having the ceremony in a house of worship you are not a member of but may want someone, other than the resident clergy to preside at your wedding, ask about the policy. Some places will not allow anyone else to perform the wedding but may allow them to participate in the ceremony. Some places will allow you to bring in your own Officiant.

FEES

What does the site fee include?_____

Is there an additional fee for ceremonies?_____

If so, cost?_____

[ ] Use of the facility

[ ] Candelabra

[ ] Janitor

[ ] Sound system person: Name and phone number:

_____

[ ] Site coordinator: Name and phone number:

_____

Will the venue allow you to also bring in your own wedding coordinator?   [ ] Yes [ ] NO

If they will, who will run the rehearsal? The site coordinator or your wedding coordinator?

_____

_____

[ ] Officiant: Name and phone Number: _____

Is fee included in the fee for using the house of worship? If not, what amount do you want to give him/her? Generally you want to put cash into an envelope to present to them afterwards. (Your wedding coordinator or best man can take care of this for you. An amount between $150 – 300 is generally the gratuity most couples give. For example, if the Officiant has also been doing pre-marital counseling with you may wish to give more than if they just perform the ceremony.)

Fee:_____

[ ] How long before the ceremony can you arrive to set up and get ready?_____

[ ] Does the facility have adequate areas for bride and attendants to dress?   [ ] Yes [ ] No
Most of the time the groom and groomsmen will arrive already dressed. If they want to change at the ceremony site, where will they dress?

[ ] Does the facility allow alcohol in the dressing areas such as Champaign?   [ ] Yes [ ] No
Some will, some won't. Be sure to ask.

ATTIRE:

If you are being married in a house of worship, inquire if there are regulations as to the type of wedding gown you can wear. Some churches/synagogues do not allow strapless dresses or for your shoulders and arms to show. Check before you start your shopping. Inquire if you do want to wear a strapless, is it acceptable to wear a shawl or jacket over your dress? Ask the same questions regarding your attendants.

MUSIC

[ ] Do you have to use the resident organist/pianist? If so are their fees included in the cost of the facility or separate?_____

_____

Name and phone number of musician:_____

_____

_____

Is there an additional fee for them to accompany the soloist(s)?

_____

Additional amount:_____

_____

[ ] Outside musicians [ ] harpist - Name and phone number:

_____

[ ] String trio/quarter : Contact and phone number:

_____

_____

Cost?

_____

[ ] Trumpet player : Contact and phone number:

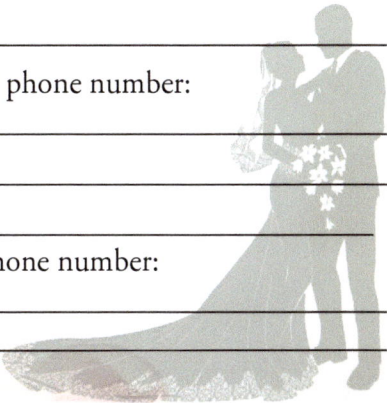

_____

_____

Cost:_____

[ ] Other music: Contact and phone number:

_____

_____

[ ] If using CDs: Who will operate player?

_____

_____

[ ] Soloist(s): Name and phone number:_____

Do they charge to sing? If so, how much?_____

Music you want played:_____

_____

_____

Do you need to provide the music or will the musician(s) provide it?

_____

If you are providing, where will you get the music?

_____

How soon does the musicians need the music?_____

If the musicians are playing for soloist(s), when will they practice?

_____

Where will they practice?_____

Does the facility allow only specific music? [ ] Yes [ ] No

If it does, get a copy of what is allowed and listen to the music to make your selections.

If the facility allows secular music, make sure it is appropriate for a wedding. Some lyrics are best saved for the reception. If in doubt, ask your coordinator or Officiant.

PRE-MARITAL COUNSELING

Does the Officiant require counseling? [ ] Yes [ ] No

If so, do they conduct the counseling? [ ] Yes [ ] No

Where:_____

When:_____

Cost(if any):_____

If you have premarital counseling outside the house of worship:

Who will counsel? Name and number_____

Cost?_____

Premarital counseling is a good idea for just about everyone. What it does is helps a couple prepare for possible problems and situations. It also is a great way to get to know each other better, especially if certain subjects are hard to discuss.

CEREMONY DÉCOR

Does the facility allow aisle runners? [ ] Yes [ ] No

Does the facility provide the aisle runner? [ ] Yes [ ] No

Who will provide the runner? You or your florist?_____

Will you have it put down ahead of time? (This is the safest way to utilize a runner, then you tie off the back of the aisle and only untie the ribbon when the mother are ready to walk in.)

Do you want a plain white runner?_____

Or a Hand decorated one? These are more expensive, but become an heirloom and a beautiful decoration in your new home.

If using an aisle runner, who will unroll it?_____

Length of Aisle:_____

When?_____

It's a good idea to consider having the florist unroll and stabilize the runner, then you know it will be safe to walk on. You don't want to catch a shoe and trip on the way down the aisle! In this case, you would tie off the aisle and have guests seated from the outside. The ribbon would be removed for the mothers to start the processional .

Do they allow petals to be dropped? [ ] Yes [ ] No

If you are using a huppa or mandap, who is responsible for decorating it?

_____

If you are going to have the facility decorated, how many pews are there?

_____

Generally you want to put pew décor on every other pew, starting with the parents' pews.

Pew

Décor:_____

Are you planning to tie off any of the rows of pews or chairs? Yes [ ] No [ ]

Will you be giving out "Seated behind the rope" cards? Yes [ ] No [ ]

If so, you will need to inform your ushers they can expect to be given the cards before being seated.

Who will be seated in the reserved section?

Parents   [ ]   Step Parents [ ]
Siblings   [ ]
Grandparents [ ]
Aunts and Uncles [ ]
Special friends [ ]
God-parents   [ ]

Others:_____

_____

Who is responsible for decorating? Florist [ ] Friends and Family [ ]

Who is responsible for taking down décor?

_____

Who is responsible for decorating? Florist [ ] Friends and Family [ ]

Who is responsible for taking down décor?

Do you want to keep any of the pew décor? [ ] Yes [ ] No

If not, who do you want to have it, providing it isn't disposable? (Such as bows)

_____

Altar Décor:
Arrangements for candelabra (usually matches the pew décor)

_____

_____

Arrangement for altar:_____

_____

Memoryflower?_____

Unity Candle: (This can also be made so it replaces an additional altar arrangement) _____

Mother Mary's Flowers: _____

_____

Where should the personal flowers be put upon delivery?

_____

See the Flowers section for additional floral details.

Do you need to provide any of the candles for the candelabra? [ ] Yes [ ] No

If so, how many?_____Do they need to be dripless? [ ] Yes [ ] No

Memory candle?_____

Who is going to light the candelabra and any other candles outside the Unity Candle?

_____

What are they going to use to light the candles? Does the facility offer candle lighters? [ ] Yes [ ] No

If you decide to have the candle lighters carry candles, buy 2 -14" tapers (dripless) for them to carry. Put a wax catcher (can be purchased at a hobby store or through your coordinator) to catch any hot wax that may drip while lighting the candles.

Are the mothers going to light the tapers by the Unity Candle? Yes[ ] No[ ]

When will they do this? As soon as they have both been escorted in [ ] Yes [ ] No

Just before the couple lights the Unity Candle [ ] Yes [ ] No

Just a note here: It's generally a lot smoother to have the mothers light the tapers when they are first escorted in, just before the groom makes his entrance.

DO light the tapers and Unity Candle ahead of time to be sure they will light for the ceremony. The same goes for any other candles, except for Paradise Candles, which once lit, are very hard to relight. By letting the candles burn for a couple of minutes, you will be assured there won't be any embarrassing moments during the ceremony because the candles don't light.

Who is responsible for the arrangements, pew décor and Unity Candle after the ceremony?_____

If you want to use any of the arrangements at the reception, who is responsible for taking and setting up?

Where do you want the arrangements placed at the reception:_____

Who is responsible for gathering up all the bride's belongings after the ceremony?_____

Where are they to be taken?_____
(Hotel or home)

Who is responsible for gathering up all the groom's belongings after the ceremony?_____

If using a limo or other form of transportation, who are they?

_____

Transportation Contact and Phone Number:_____
Who is to call and at what time, in case the limo is late?

_____

What is your back up if the limo doesn't show?_____
_____

Unfortunately this does happen. Don't let it ruin your day, have a plan in place just in case it does happen. This can be eliminated if you use a reputable limo service.

If gifts are brought to the ceremony, who is responsible for transporting Gifts to the reception?_____

(If you have a wedding coordinator, they will take care of all the above situations from gathering up the belongings to follow up with the limo.

Time Line: What time will you arrive at the ceremony site?_____

Are you having your hair or make-up done on site?_____

When you do need to be done with hair and make-up to start pictures?
_____

> Allow at least 1½ hours before ceremony for pictures, especially since pictures should be concluded ½ hour prior to the start of the ceremony.

Will attendants and flower-girl(s) arrive at the same time as the bride?
_____

Time Groom/groomsmen/ring bearer arrive?_____

Parents arrive?_____

Grandparents arrive?_____

Time photographer and videographer are to arrive:_____

Be sure to give your photographer and videographer a list of pictures you want. (See the Photo Section for ideas.)

It's important that you have your photographer and videographer speak with the officials at the house of worship where you are getting married to be sure they know the rules. Otherwise, there may be some very uncomfortable moments if they arrive and find they can't set up just anywhere they want to.

Are you seeing each other before the wedding? [ ] Yes [ ] No

If not, allow time for separate pictures to be done. This also cuts down on the length of time needed after the ceremony for pictures as you'll just be doing the "combined" pictures.

Time Florist is to arrive to decorate:

_____

Time Musicians/Soloists/ Readers are to arrive:

_____

Time Guest book attendant arrives:

_____

Ushers arrive:_____

Officiant arrives:_____

Ask if you can leave your dress, (unless the coordinator is delivering it to you), attendants' attire, guest book, Unity Candle, and anything else for the ceremony at the facility the night before. If you can, bring to the rehearsal (if you are having one.) **DON'T FORGET YOUR MARRIAGE LICENSE and RINGS.**

It's also a good idea to have a copy of the ceremony (just in case) and copies of any readings being done.

Who is responsible for the floral arrangements, pew décor and unity candle after the ceremony?

_____

(If you are utilizing a wedding coordinator, they should be taking care of these items for you.)

Who is responsible for the floral arrangements, pew décor and unity candle after the ceremony?

_____

_____

Are you going to pass out bubbles or something else for when you exit the ceremony site?

What are you using?_____Who is going to hand out?_____

Be sure to check with the facility as to what they will allow to be used. Some ideas are bubbles, confetti, latex balloons, doves, flower petals, Flutter Fettie™

For ideas for readings and scriptures refer to **the Miscellaneous** section of this book.

Do the ushers know how to perform their duties? If not, who is going to show them how to usher?

_____

Will the ushers be handing out the programs? If not, who is responsible to do this?

_____

Additional items you may want to have on hand:

- Bible or Talmud (or copy of any other holy book being used for the ceremony)
- Umbrellas if the ceremony is to take place outdoors and it is expected to be hot, especially for elderly guests.
- Ice water for guests to sip on during ceremony if it's hot.
- Ice and towels in case anyone passes out during the ceremony.
- Remember to have your attendants scuff their shoes if they are new, so they don't slip walking down the aisle.
- If having a longer ceremony, in the sun, out of doors, consider placing chairs so attendants can be seated. This will help keep any of them from fainting from standing for to long in the heat. (Especially if the ceremony is being held at a higher elevation than they may be used to.

What time do you want the photos to be finished?_____

Time you want to leave for the reception:_____

Ideally, your "after ceremony" pictures, should take no longer than 30 – 45 minutes.

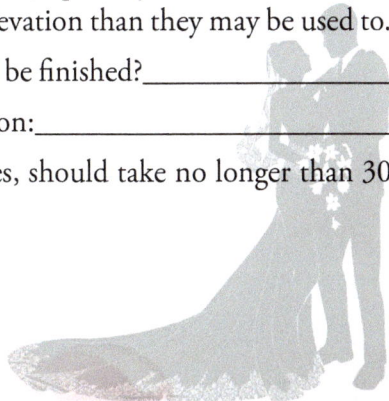

RECEPTION

(TO AVOID ANY MISUNDERSTANDINGS, CAREFULLY READ ALL CONTRACTS BEFORE SIGNING- ASK FOR EVERYTHING TO BE PUT IN WRITING SO THERE IS NO MISUNDERSTANDINGS. IT'S A GOOD IDEA TO HAVE YOUR COORDINATOR LOOK OVER THE CONTRACT)

Site:_____

Date available:_____

Rental Price:_____

Cancellation policy:_____

Type of reception:Cake & coffee/punch; Hors d'oeuvres; Buffet; Sit-down-dinner; Garden/Outdoors

Other_____

Included at facility:

[ ] Linens [ ] Skirting [ ] Floor length table cloths [ ] Tables [ ] 5' [ ] 6'

[ ] Chairs   [ ] Security   [ ]Decorative items

[ ] Chair covers   [ ] Table Mirrors/Votive Candles

Ample parking?_____

Distance from ceremony:_____

Child Care:_____

Catering requirements:_____

In-house:_____

Outside:_____

Number of restrooms?:_____

Handicapped accessible?_____

Hours available:_____

Caterer:_____

Pricing system:_____

Cancellation policy:

_____

Per item:_____

Labor charges:_____

Delivery charge:_____

Plate charge:_____

Menu Format:

Buffet:_____

_____

Sit-down meal:_____

_____

_____

What about special dinners, ex. vegetarian:_____

Coffee/cake/punch:_____

Number of guests invited:_____

Decorations for Reception:_____

_____

Who will decorate?_____

_____

Baker:_____

Wedding cake:_____

Grooms cake:_____

Florist:_____

MUSIC

Band [ ] Orchestra [ ] DJ [ ]

It is a good idea to provide a meal for the vendors who will be at all the function such as the Coordinator, Photographer, Videographer and DJ

Have refreshments available for members of a band. Where will they eat?

_____

Are there any restrictions on music or hours?

TYPES OF MUSIC:

Rock and Roll [ ] Country [ ] Mood [ ] Classical [ ] Combination [ ] Swing [ ]

Name of Group:_____

Fee: $_____ Deposit:$ _____ DUE: _____

Number of breaks:_____ Length of breaks:_____

Accepts requests:_____ Will be Master of Ceremonies:_____

(Do they dress appropriately?)

Special music you may want to request:

Dinner music:_____

CHOSEN MUSIC SELECTIONS

First Dance:_____

Bride/Father's Dance:_____

Groom/Mother's Dance:_____

Cake Cutting:_____

Tossing the Bouquet:_____

Tossing the Garter:_____

Last Dance before leaving on Honeymoon:_____

Your favorite songs:_____

_____

_____

BAR

Bartender(s):_____

Will prices for reception site/menu etc. be guaranteed for wedding date?_____

Restrictions:_____

_____

NOTES:

Questions to ask hotel/caterer.

1. Be sure EVERYTHING is in writing. Don't leave anything to chance or memory.

2. What does the room charge include? It it room rental only or is it the minimums of food and beverage?

3. Be sure you know what is charged for and what is included.

4. Will they guarantee prices if the wedding date is several months away?

5. What do they provide? Is there an extra cost?

   a. Person to cut and serve cake?

   b. What items do you include for decorating? Is there a charge for these items?

6. Will they set up a tasting? Is there a charge for this?

7. How early can you set up?

   When does it need to be dismantled?

8. Is there storage for items such as flowers you may bring in to decorate with.

9. Do they allow you to bring in your own champagne? Is there a corking fee?

10. Tables --what do they provide?

    1. Gift table/guest book

    2. Cake table

11. Table, seating arrangements.

    Head table (More and more brides are getting away from the traditional "head table" and opting for more reserved tables for the wedding party.

    Some couples prefer a "Sweetheart's Table" where only the Bride and Groom are seated, and their honor attendants seated at tables close by.

    Are you going to designate seating?

(If step-parent situation, do you need separate tables for each family?)

12. Bar

    1.   Open

    2.   Hosted

    a.   Do they provide bartenders? Charge.

13. What is the ration of waiters to guests?

(You don't want to few, or the service won't be as good.)

14. Is a champagne toast included in the total price of the reception?

15. Where do they store the top layer of the cake and cake top? You someone pick it up the next day? (May want to designate someone to pick it up right after the reception... possibly sister, maid of honor/mother.) (Check with pastry shop to see if they provide a complimentary cake for your first anniversary. This way the entire cake can be served at the wedding.)

16. If they are providing any additional services such as ordering flowers or other decorations, etc. for the reception what is their charge? (Usually they'll charge an additional 20% for this service.) It may be better to arrange this yourself.

17. Parking services...is there a charge?_____

18. What time will the DJ/Band be setting up?_____

19. Special pricing for guest rooms?_____

20. Will there be more than my reception going on? How many functions will you be working with at the same time?

21. What linens does the caterer supply? Do they have various colors? What about chair covers? If they don't have them, will they rent them for you?

NOTES:

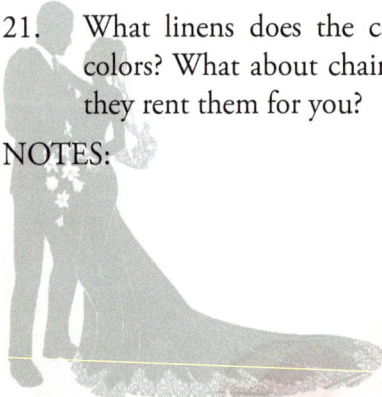

WEDDING RECEPTION
Suggested Timetable

First hour:
  Music begins
  Guest start arriving at reception
  Bar opens and Hors d'oeuvres are served

After First 45 minutes
  Dinner is announced and guests are seated.
  DJ or Band Director announces bride and groom
  Bride's father (or whoever is the host) gives a welcome
  Blessing is offered – if this is to be done
  Music can resume during dinner

After Bride and Groom finish their meal
  Bride and Groom may choose to circulate among guests while guests finish eating

After 2 hours
  Tables are cleared Cake cutting ceremony
  Attendants and ushers line up on either side of table.
  Bride and groom share first piece together
  Next pieces of cake are served to bride's and groom's parents
  Guests are served.
  Dance music and first dance is announced for bride and groom.
  Father/Daughter dance
  Mother/Son Dance
      (Keep these two dances to about two to three (2-3) minutes so guests won't get bored. Get your guests on the dance floor as soon as possible.)

After 2 hours
  Close bar
  Offer non-alcoholic beverages to guests

After 2 hours
  Bride and groom change in to going-away clothes (if leaving directly from the reception on the honeymoon) and say goodbye to parents.
  Bride and groom may choose to have a "last dance"
  Guests gather to toss rice, bubbles, flowers, etc. as B/G leave.

(This can also be done when B/G leave church before the reception.)
Parents signal band and bar when they are ready to leave.
Parents bid good night to guests.

*The bouquet and garter toss can take place anytime after the cake cutting. After the cake is cut, guests may feel free to leave the reception. The longer the wait to do the tosses, the less the number of guests who may be available to participate.

NOTES:

RECEIVING LINE

TRADITIONAL ORDER:

Facing from right to left:

Bride's mother (far right) Groom's mother

Groom's father Bride

Groom

Maid of honor Attendants Ushers (optional

Bride's father (optional) he usually mingles with guests.

Traditional Formal order:

Bride's Mother Groom's mother
Bride
Groom
Maid of Honor
Bridesmaids (optional)

Semi-Formal

Bride's mother
Bride's Father
Bride
Groom
Groom's Mother
Groom's Father

More couples are choosing not to do the traditional receiving line. Instead here are some options you may consider.

Consider returning to the altar area and dismissing your guests, instead of having the ushers do it, row by row.

Make the rounds to the tables to visit with each guest at the reception.

Have a Farewell Circle. This is where the guests form a circle around the couple, usually on the dance floor. At a starting point, the bride goes one way, the groom the other. They greet each guest as they walk around the circle. Once the B/G have completed the circle, they depart.

Have a Farewell Arch. This is where the guests form an arch by forming two lines and joining hands overhead. The couple then proceeds through the arch and out the door.

PLACE CARDS AND SEATING ASSIGNMENTS

NAME	TABLE NUMBER	NAME	TABLE NUMBER

PLACE CARDS AND SEATING ASSIGNMENTS

NAME	TABLE NUMBER	NAME	TABLE NUMBER

<u>**Different Hotel Packages:**</u>

ARRANGEMENTS FOR OUT OF TOWN GUESTS:
Transportation from airport/train etc. to hotel:
_____

Where will they stay? What will they do?
_____
_____
_____
_____
_____
_____

Children's Activities:

Babysitters:

GRATUITIES

Person(s)to Tip	Tip Rate/Amount	By whom/when
Baker Florist	1-20% of total only for very special service.(A tip is not expected but is appropriate if work is exceptional.)	Add to bill at time of payment
Photographer Videographer	Send a Thank Yor they can use as a reference for their work	
Wedding Consultant	Tip 1-20% of total only for special service.	Add to tip at time of payment
Caterer	Tip 1-20% OF TOTAL FOR SPECIAL SERVICE.	Add to tip at time of payment
Musicians	Tip $10/per person and up Depending on service	
Club Manager	If gratuity is not included in fee, tip 15-20%	
Bartenders Table Captain Waiters/waitresses *(Tip is usually included. Ask to be sure.)*	If Gratuity is not included in bill, tip is usually give 15-20% of total bill to maitre d', hotel or captain to distribute to staff	Add to bill at time of payment
Coat/Powder Room Attendants in Hotels/Clubs	Either flat fee prearranged with hotel/club or pay about $1.00 per guest to staff	Flat fee added to bill (Request signs be set out informing guests gratuity is paid.)
Limo/Carriage Drivers	Tip is 20% of total Bill and usually included in total cost. (Ask to be certain.)	Ceremony host pays driver(s) directly at reception site.
Civil Ceremony Official, (Judge, J.P.)	Usually charge a flat fee. Some judges may not be allowed to accept money for service. Ask prior to arranging the ceremony.	Best man pays Officiant after ceremony. Groom gives money to best man before the service.
Clergy (Pastor, Priest, Minister, Rabbi, etc.)	Usually a donation. Amount depends on size of ceremony. Ask prior to arranging ceremony.	Best man pays Officiant after ceremony. Groom gives money to best man before the service.

Car Valet	Tip $1-$2 per car	If valet is hosted, request valet inform guests gratuity is being taken care of by host.
Skycaps/Bellhops Doorman	Tip 50 cents to $1 for each bag handled.	Paid by husband or wife
Hotel (Chambermaid)	Typically tip $1-2 per day; for very special service.	Leave tip in envelope on dresser.

[ ] Envelopes to put gratuities in for distribution.

** If you aren't comfortable in giving a cash tip to vendors but would like to show your appreciation for a job well done, consider sending a gift basket or a gift certificate along with a thank-you they can use for references.

GUEST LIST

NAME&ADDRESS	PHONE	CEREMON	RECEPTION	RSVP	ANNOUNCEMENT	THANKYOU

GUEST LIST

NAME&ADDRESS	PHONE	CEREMON	RECEPTION	RSVP	ANNOUNCEMENT	THANKYOU

GUEST LIST

NAME & ADDRESS	PHONE	CEREMON	RECEPTION	RSVP	ANNOUNCEMENT	THANKYOU

GUEST LIST

NAME & ADDRESS	PHONE	CEREMON	RECEPTION	RSVP	ANNOUNCEMENT	THANKYOU

GUEST LIST

NAME & ADDRESS	PHONE	CEREMON	RECEPTION	RSVP	ANNOUNCEMENT	THANKYOU

TRANSPORTATION/HOTEL ARRANGEMENTS FOR OUT OF TOWN GUESTS

Assign the responsibility of getting out of town guests around to someone who is familiar with the area

If your guests are staying at different hotels, you may wish to arrange for a van to pick them all up and transport them to the location of your wedding then on to the reception if it is not at the same location.

Another idea may be to rent a double-decker bus to take everyone on to the reception!

Guest	Airline	Arrival Date	Arrival Date	Hotel	Reservations Made by	Departure Time	Departure Time	Car Rental/ Transport

YOUR HONEYMOON

Your first trip together as husband and wife should be one that you will remember, with good memories, all your life. Discuss together what your expectations are as where you'd like to go and what you'd like to do?

Determine how much you can spend.

Transportation expense, (air, train, ship etc.)_____

Do you want an all inclusive resort?_____

> All inclusive usually includes all meals, drinks, room and entertainment. (When researching, be sure to ask exactly what is included.

> Sandles™ is one of the popular resorts for honeymoons. There are many more. Find a good travel agent you are comfortable with and let them do the foot work if you don't have the time. You may find some better deals if you go on-line and do the research yourself, especially if you can make your reservations ahead of time.

Who is paying for your honeymoon? Groom [ ] Family [ ]

What do you want to do? Some ideas might be…

> Lying on a beach
> Swimming in the ocean
> Skiing in the mountains
> Camping in the mountains
> Camping in Hawaii
> Touring a foreign country
> Snorkeling and scuba diving
> Sight seeing
> Fishing
> Biking
> Hang Gliding
> Cruising on a ship
> Great dining
> Dog Sledding

Sleigh Rides
Golf
Someplace that offers a spa
Whale watching
Make sure you select a place where there will be something for both of you to do.

Some popular honeymoon places:
Hawaii
Costa Rica
Europe
Caribbean Islands
Jamaica
Fiji
Australia
Tahiti
Canadian Rockies
Rocky Mountains
Yellowstone National Park
Yosemite National Park
Mexico
Alaska
Any place in the U.S.
Disney World

Check out any company you decide to work with before giving them a deposit. Be sure they are reputable and will stand behind what they promise. Talk to other couples who have trav-eled to any place you are planning on visiting. Ask for suggestions for dining, lodging, etc. Notes:

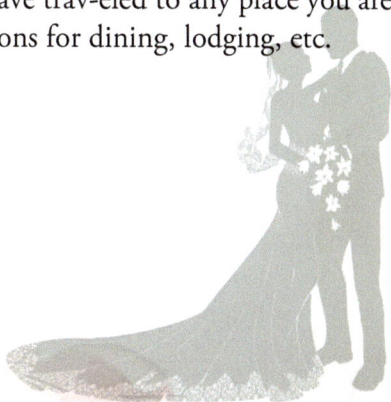

THE REGISTRY

Before you register, take time to make a list of what you have and what you need. If you have never set up a household, then you are going to need everything!

When you register, keep in mind everyone you will be inviting. You want to select items for your registry in all price points.

Some items you may want to consider registering for are:

Kitchen

[ ] Bake Ware – Cookie pans, cake pans, pie pans
[ ] Bar utensils
[ ] Blender
[ ] Butter Dish
[ ] Can Opener
[ ] Cook books
[ ] Cook Ware – A good set of pots and pans
[ ] Cookie Jar
[ ] Cutting Board
[ ] Dish clothes/towels
[ ] Dish drainer
[ ] Everyday dishes
[ ] Hand Mixer
[ ] Peppermill
[ ] Pitchers
[ ] Placemats and Napkins

[ ] Rolling Pen
[ ] Bar glass wear
[ ] Skillet
[ ] Serving Dishes
[ ] Spice Rack
[ ] Cookie cutters
[ ] Cooking/Serving Utensils
[ ] Pizza Pan with Cutter
[ ] Drinking Glasses
[ ] Hot pads
[ ] Mixing Bowls
[ ] Stainless Silverware
[ ] Toaster or Toasting Oven
[ ] Coffee maker
[ ] Measuring Spoons and Cups
[ ] Salt and Pepper shakers

Bedroom

[ ] 4 blankets

[ ] Sheets/pillow cases – 2 sets

[ ] Comforter/bed skirt, pillow shams
[ ] 4 pillows

Bathroom

[ ] Bath rug
[ ] Toothbrush holder
[ ] Towel sets – Bath, hand and washcloth
[ ] Weight Scale

[ ] Toilet Cover/rug
[ ] Kleenex box
[ ] Soap dish
[ ] Bath Mat

Dining Room

[ ] Table clothes with napkins   [ ] Silver or Good Stainless Silverware
[ ] China   [ ] Crystal salad bowl
[ ] Pair of Crystal candlesticks   [ ] Vase
[ ] Trivets   [ ] Serving dishes
[ ] Crystal salt and pepper shakers [ ] Dessert dishes
[ ] Crystal – Water/red and white wine

Additional Suggestions

[ ] Tool kit   [ ] Gardening tools
[ ] Fireplace tools   [ ] Decorative items
[ ] Board games   [ ] Camping Equipment
[ ] Picnic Basket   [ ] Ice Cream Maker

This list is meant too get you started. You will have additional items that you find you'd like to have. Try to register at places where it will be easy for guests to select items on line if necessary.

Some stores you might consider:

American Furniture
Bed, Bath and Beyond
Crate and Barrel
Dillard's
Home Depot
International Villa
J.C. Penney
Macy's
REI
Target
Wal-Mart
William Sanoma

You do not need to limit yourself to one or two stores. If possible, set aside a time when you and your fiancé can go together to select the items for your home.

Once you have made your selections and registered, put this information on your website and give it to both families. Do not put registry information in your save the dates or invitations. If you do, it may appear that you are asking for a gift.

Do check with the stores regarding their exchange policies. Also, inquire if there is any guarantee that the items you select will be in stock. Select china that is "open stock". This way you are assured you will be able to add to your pattern.

General Marriage License Requirements

You need to check with the County Clerk in the town or city where you plan to be married as each State had different laws that apply.

Both bride and groom **must apply in person** for your license. You'll need to take one form of identification that shows your date of birth and social security number.

Most County Clerks WILL NOT accept checks or credit cards. Check with them.

ACCEPTED IDENTIFICATION –

Valid Driver's License
Birth Certificate
Passport
Visa, Military ID

Be sure to take your Social Security Card.

General Marriage License Requirements

For general information only.

STATE	AGE	COSTS VARY STATE TO STATE	WAITING PERIOD	WAITING PERIOD IF DIVORCED	HOW LONG LICENSE IS GOOD FOR	BLOOD TEST REQUIRED
Alabama	18	$28- 41	None	6 months	30 Days	None
Alaska	18	$25	3 Days	Proof	90 Days	None
Arizona	18	$50	None		1 Year	None
Arkansas	18	$35	None		60 Days	None
California	18	$80	None	Proof	90 Days	None
Colorado	18	$10	None	Date,County, Stat	30 Days	None
Connecticut	18	$35	None		65 Days	Yes
Delaware	18	$35	1 day- residents 4 if not		30 Days	None
District of Columbia	18	$95	5 Days	Proof	No Expiration	Yes
Florida	18	$88.50 $56 if couple takes 4 hr. course	0 – 3 Days	Date of Divorce or Death	60 Days	None
Georgia	18	$26+	None	Proof	No Expiration	Yes
Hawaii	18	$50	None		30 Days	None
Idaho	18	$28	None		No Expiration	None
Illinois	18	$15-30	1 Day	Proof	60 Days	Yes
Indiana	18	$18-$60	None	Proof	60 Days	None
Iowa	18	$30	3 Days	Final Filed	6 Months	None
Kansas	18	$75	3 Days	How marriage Ended	None	None
Kentucky	18	$34.50	None		30 Days	None
Louisiana	18	$25+	72 Hrs.	Proof	30 Days	None
Maine	18	$20	None	Proof	90 Days	None
Maryland	18	$35+	2 Days	Proof	6 Months	None

Massachusetts	18	$4+	3 Days	Must be sure Divorce is Absolute	60 days	Yes
Michigan	18	$20-30	3 Days		33 Days	None
Minnesota	18	$70	5 Days		6 Months	None
Mississippi	18	$22	None	Proof	30 Days	Yes
Missouri	18	$50	3 Days	Proof	30 Days	None
Montana	18	$30.25	None		6 Months	Yes
Nebraska	18	$15	None	Date Ended	1 Year	None
Nevada	18	$35-42	None	Date, City, State	1 Year	None
New Hampshire	18	$45	3 Days	Proof	90 Days	None
New Jersey	18	$28	3 Days	Proof	30 Days	None
New Mexico	18	$25-40	None		No Expiration	None
New York	18	$25-30	24 Hrs.	Proof	60 Days	None

Please call your town//county/city clerk to request details about specific requirements well ahead of time so you will be prepared. They will answer any additional questions you may have. Please note that most states will only accept cash in payment of Marriage Licenses.

Proof of Divorce or Death of previous spouse varies from state to state. Call your County Clerk's office for specific documents you may need to take with you.

CHANGING YOUR NAME

If you take your husband's name after marriage, you will need to notify the following about your name change. You will also need certified copies of your license to submit for name change.

[ ] Credit Card Companies
[ ] Department of Motor Vehicles (license and Registration)
[ ] Checking Account
[ ] Savings Account
[ ] IRA Account (Pension Plans)
[ ] Insurance Companies
[ ] Mortgagee Companies
[ ] Employer/School
[ ] Investment Companies (Stocks, Bonds)
[ ] Wills and Beneficiaries
[ ] Family Tree Entry
[ ] Social Security
[ ] Voter Registration
[ ] Newspaper and Magazine Subscriptions
[ ] Doctors
[ ] Dentists
[ ] Library Card
[ ] Clubs/Memberships
[ ] Passport
[ ] Post Office
[ ] Electric/Gas Co.
[ ] Water Co.
[ ] Telephone Co.
[ ] Garbage Co.
[ ] Business Associates (Business Cards)
[ ] Family and Friends

Take care of this as soon as possible after the wedding.

SUGGESTED SCRIPTURES FOR WEDDING

Old Testament
  Genesis 2:20-24
  Ruth 1:16-17
  Ecclesiastics 3:1-8
  Song of Solomon 2:10-13; 4:9-12; 8:6-7; 5:9-16
  Proverbs 3:10-31

New Testament
  Matthew 19:4-6
  John 2:1-10
  1 Corinthians 8:2; 13:1-13
  Ephesians 5:22-33
  1 Peter 3:1-7

SUGGESTED READINGS/POEMS

Selected Verses from **THE PROPHET** by Kahil Gibran
RED, RED ROSE by *Burns*
THE PASSIONATE SHEPARD TO HIS LOVE by *Christopher Marlowe*
THE OBLIGATION by *Swinburne*
MAN WANTS BUT LITTLE by *John Quincy Adams*
SONNETS FROM THE PORTUGUESE (HOW DO I LOVE THEE?) by *Elizabeth Barrett Browning*
LOVE'S PHILOSOPHY by *Percy Byshe Shelley*
SONNET CXVI by *William Shakespeare*
WEDDING BLESSINGS by *June Cotner (Prayers and Poems)*
INTO THE GARDEN A WEDDING ANTHOLOGY, *Robert Hass & Stephen Mitchell (A collection of Poetry and Prose on Love and Marriage)*

List of your favorite Scriptures and Poems

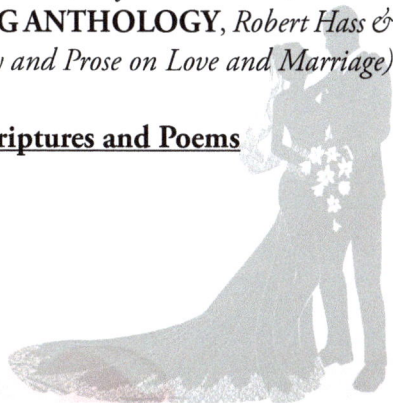

TIPS AND MONEY SAVING IDEAS

If you are working with a limited budget, consider some of these tips to help save money. Forgo the Champagne – Use Sparkling Cider or the beverage being served with the meal.

If you want a large cake for show, consider having an artificial cake decorated. Have only the top cake be real so you can cut it. Serve your guests sheet cakes.

Decorate with lots of bows and tulle. These go a long way in stretching a budget.

Use centerpieces provided by the reception site. For example,, mirrors, bowls for floating candles or flowers, votive candles.

Utilize flowers that are in season.

Get married during a holiday like Christmas. Most churches and reception sites are all ready decorated.

Check out pricing of plated dinners before settling on buffets. It may cost less, as less food needs to be prepared.

Use family candleholders for your unity candle tapers. They'll all sentiment and you can pass them on to your own children when they get married.

Buy Toasting Glasses in the crystal pattern you want to have. Have the two glasses engraved with your monogram and date – then use them after the wedding!

Instead of spending money on favors people will probably never use, consider making a contribution to a favorite charity.

Consider having your wedding and reception at a facility that is full service. They offer flowers, catering, DJ, cake etc. Some even include the Officiant and DJ.

Arrange for your ceremony and reception flowers to be given to a hospital, hospice, or nursing home. They love to receive them and distribute the flowers to the patients and you don't have to worry about what wasting the flowers.

Arrange for your Maid of Honor and Best Man to take your dress to the cleaners and return the tuxes.

Arrange to have some finger foods at the ceremony site to nibble on before the wedding. It's important that everyone have something in their stomach before they march down the aisle. Don't forget soft drinks and water. Grapes, cold cuts, cheese and sliced fruit are good and not messy.

EMERGENCY KITS

One thing about a wedding is to expect the unexpected. Be prepared for anything that may crop up. Here's a list of things to put into a case to take along with you. (Put your maid of honor or someone in charge of it.) If you have a coordinator, they will usually supply the emergency kit.

Advil and Tylenol	Pepto-Bismol
Emery Board	Nail repair kit
Extra Nylons	Nail polish to match your nailsl
Hair brush	Hair Spray
Hairpins	Breath mints
Hard candy	Lip gloss or Vaseline
Kleenex	Make up kit
Matches	Band-Aids
Scotch Tape	An Extra pen with black ink
Steamer	Imitation rings for ring pillow
Toothbrush(s)	Tooth Paste

Needle and thread with thread in white, black and matching colors of attendant's attire

IDEAS FOR FAVORS

♥A favor is something you give your guests to say Thank You for helping us celebrate our special day. It can be as simple as candy tied in tulle, a live Colorado Blue Spruce Tree or a silver picture frame. ♥

♥Tie Silver and Gold Hershey kisses in tulle and tie with a ribbon.

♥Have powdered hot chocolate mix packaged in bags and tie with a ribbon.

♥Put coffee beans in tulle and tie with a ribbon.

♥Put two or more flower bulbs, nestled in "straw" in a pretty box, for your guests to take home and plant.

♥Give guests a Colorado Blue Spruce to take home and plant.

♥Use small picture frams as place cards. Calligraphy the guest's name on the frame then they can use it later for pictures. You can also put your engagement picture in it and have their place card inserted on top of it. These frames can be silver-plated, silver, porcelain or whatever works with your style of wedding.

Give each guest a bell to ring as you leave the ceremony. They then take it to the reception to ring when they want
you to kiss.

♥Have a silver bell at each place setting for guests to ring when they want you to kiss then is their's to take home.

♥Have Fortune Cookies made. You can put special messages in each for your guests.

♥Purchase pretty votive candleholders, put a scented candle in it and wrap in tulle, tied with a ribbon.

♥Put a plate of special chocolates on a special plate, placed on the guest's tables, to be shared when they have dessert.

♥Buy packets of flower seeds, tie tow together and place at each place setting.

♥Put a colorful fish in a bubble bowl for each guest to take home.

♥Use goldfish in your centerpieces.

♥Purchase yo-yos, have stickers made with your names and date to put on them.

♥Have homemade cookies made with your names and date.

♥Put an individual teacup and saucer with a flower arrangement at each place setting for your guests to take home.

♥If you are getting married during the Christmas season, give each guest a Christmas ornament or cookie cutter.

♥Personalize bottles of wine.

♥Have a gift bag of cookies or cheese and crakers for each guest as they leave a late reception to nibble on as they return home or to their hotel room.

♥Have a flower, complete with a pin, for each guest to pin on.

♥Have a small Christmas stocking filled with candy for each guest.

♥Use Easter Baskets for centerpieces and small baskets at each guest's place filled with candy.

♥If you travel a lot, bring back something from your travels to give. For example; if you go to Hawaii a lot, arrange for each guest to have a lei. If you go to Australia, bring back little Kolas for your guests.

♥Wrap traditional Jordan Almonds in tulle for each guest.

WHAT SHOULD WE THROW SINCE WE CAN'T USE RICE?

Birdseed   Bubbles
Confetti   Flower Petals
Give each guest a bell to ring In the Fall, use colored leaves Release balloons. Be sure they are Latex. These are environmentally friendly. Release doves If you play baseball, have your groomsmen form an "honor guard" using baseball bats. If you golf, use golf clubs, if tennis is your game, use tennis rackets, etc.

www.ingramcontent.com/pod-product-compliance
Lightning Source LLC
Chambersburg PA
CBHW040937030426
42335CB00001B/18